BICYCLE
AROUND THE WORLD

LINDA
SVENDSEN

BICYCLE
AROUND THE WORLD

GIBBS
P
SMITH

Gibbs Smith, Publisher
Salt Lake City

First Edition
06 05 04 03 02   5 4 3 2 1

Published by
Gibbs Smith, Publisher
P.O. Box 667
Layton, Utah 84041

Orders: (1-800) 748-5439
www.gibbs-smith.com

Edited by Suzanne Gibbs Taylor
Designed and produced by Kurt Wahlner
Printed and bound in Hong Kong

ISBN 1-58685-209-4

Half-Title Page: BENICIA | CALIFORNIA

Title Page: BENICIA | CALIFORNIA

Introduction

Bicycles are many things to many people. To the owners of many of the bicycles depicted here, they are central elements of life providing needed transportation to carry heavy loads . . . to most Americans, bicycles are children's toys or recreational gear . . . but to Linda Svendsen they are works of art and interest infused with the culture in which she finds them. Look behind the bicycles in her pictures and enjoy the richly textured context she presents.

Many cultures use representations of wheels as a symbol for the wholeness of life. The wheel is also the essence of the bicycle. Its hub is at the center and anchors the spokes. The spokes are thin and weak, but together they share the load on the wheel and keep the rim straight by maintaining constant, even tension. The rim and tire turn continuously, repeating the never-ending life cycle. Humans have weakness, as do the spokes in the wheel, but when we bond together in a family, we share our strengths. We give birth, nurture the young, and receive nurturing in old age, repeating the never-ending life cycle. To me the bicycle is a metaphor for balance and harmony in life—something we are all looking for. To increase them in your life, try riding your bike!

Ed Brennan
Benicia, California
June 2002

PARIS | FRANCE

Amsterdam | Netherlands

INNSBRUCK | AUSTRIA

FURTA KLASZTORNA

ZAŁATWIANIE
INTERESANTÓW
ZAMAWIANIE
MSZY ŚW.

Warsaw | Poland

Florence | Italy

KONYA | TURKEY

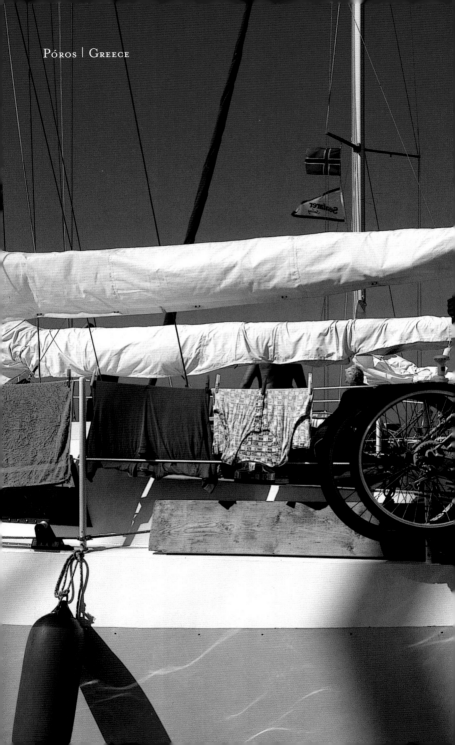

KONYA ┆ TURKEY·

Chiang Rai | Thailand

THE VALLEY OF THE KINGS | EGYPT

Java | Indonesia

Queensland | Australia

MARRAKESH | MOROCCO

McCall | Idaho

CAPE COD | MASSACHUSETTS

AMSTERDAM | NETHERLANDS

Bordeaux | France

SNCF

Le hall de la gare
un espace piéto
Pensez aux autres
conduisez vos bi
à la main pour le t

Vienna | Austria

Konya | Turkey

Jodhpur | India

STELLENBOSCH | SOUTH AFRICA

Patan | Nepal

CHIANG RAI | THAILAND

BEIJING | CHINA

Amsterdam | Netherlands

Rome | Italy

Café "Ruysdael"

Amsterdam | Netherlands

Amsterdam | Netherlands

Vienna | Austria

Nice | France

HELSINKI | FINLAND

Buenos Aires | Argentina

Benicia | California

DANVILLE | CALIFORNIA

Danville | California

Danville, California

RED ONION
SALOON
Est. 1898

Salzburg | Austria

brasserie LE FORUM bar gla

Paris | France

BAR - SNACK

LE
MARIGNAN

RESTAURANT

INNSBRUCK | AUSTRIA

Lucerne | Switzerland

Discoteca

THE **C** LUB
IL SABATO

SORRENTO

Żelazowa Wola | Poland

KONYA | TURKEY

KATHMANDU | NEPAL

BEIJING | CHINA

杭州市

寄存处

安局制

CANTON | CHINA

RIVER KWAI | THAILAND

KURANDA | AUSTRALIA

KURANDA
BOTTOM
PUB
COURTESY
Vehicle

XX

Our

EXPORT
SWAN
LAGER

SWAN
PREMIUM

JAVA | INDONESIA

Pretoria | South Africa

MARRAKESH | MOROCCO

AMSTERDAM | NETHERLANDS

BENICIA | CALIFORNIA

MT. DIABLO | CALIFORNIA.

CATALINA ISLAND | CALIFORNIA

Port Townsend | Washington

CYCLES

REPCO CYCLES & ACCESSORIES

CYCLES

574.484

Travel
Services

CHIANG RAI | THAILAND

BEIJING | CHINA

सं जूस

गाजर जूस 6-00
मैंगो शेक 7-00

GOLDLINE

Delhi | India

Konya | Turkey

FEZ | MOROCCO

Amsterdam | Netherlands

Amsterdam | Netherlands

RIO DE JANEIRO | BRAZIL

PISAC | PERU

BENICIA | CALIFORNIA

DANVILLE | CALIFORNIA

CAMBRIDGE | MASSACHUSETTS

AMSTERDAM | NETHERLANDS

Amsterdam | Netherlands

AMSTERDAM | NETHERLANDS

Carcassonne | France

SNCF

Le hall de la gare demeure
un espace piéton .
Pensez aux autres voyageurs,
conduisez vos bicyclettes
à la main pour le traverser .
Merci .

Bordeaux | France

BEIJING | CHINA

BEIJING | CHINA

River K

DO NOT
OVERTAKE
TURNING VEHICLE

The Outback | Australia

SYDNEY | AUSTRALIA

CAIRNS | AUSTRALIA

HERVEY BAY | AUSTRALIA

Jabiru
2km

Skagway | Alaska

MT. DIABLO | CALIFORNIA

Benicia | California

PROVINCETOWN | MASSACHUSETTS

New York City | New York

Pisac | Peru

LAKE COUNTRY | CHILE

Ollantaytambo | Peru

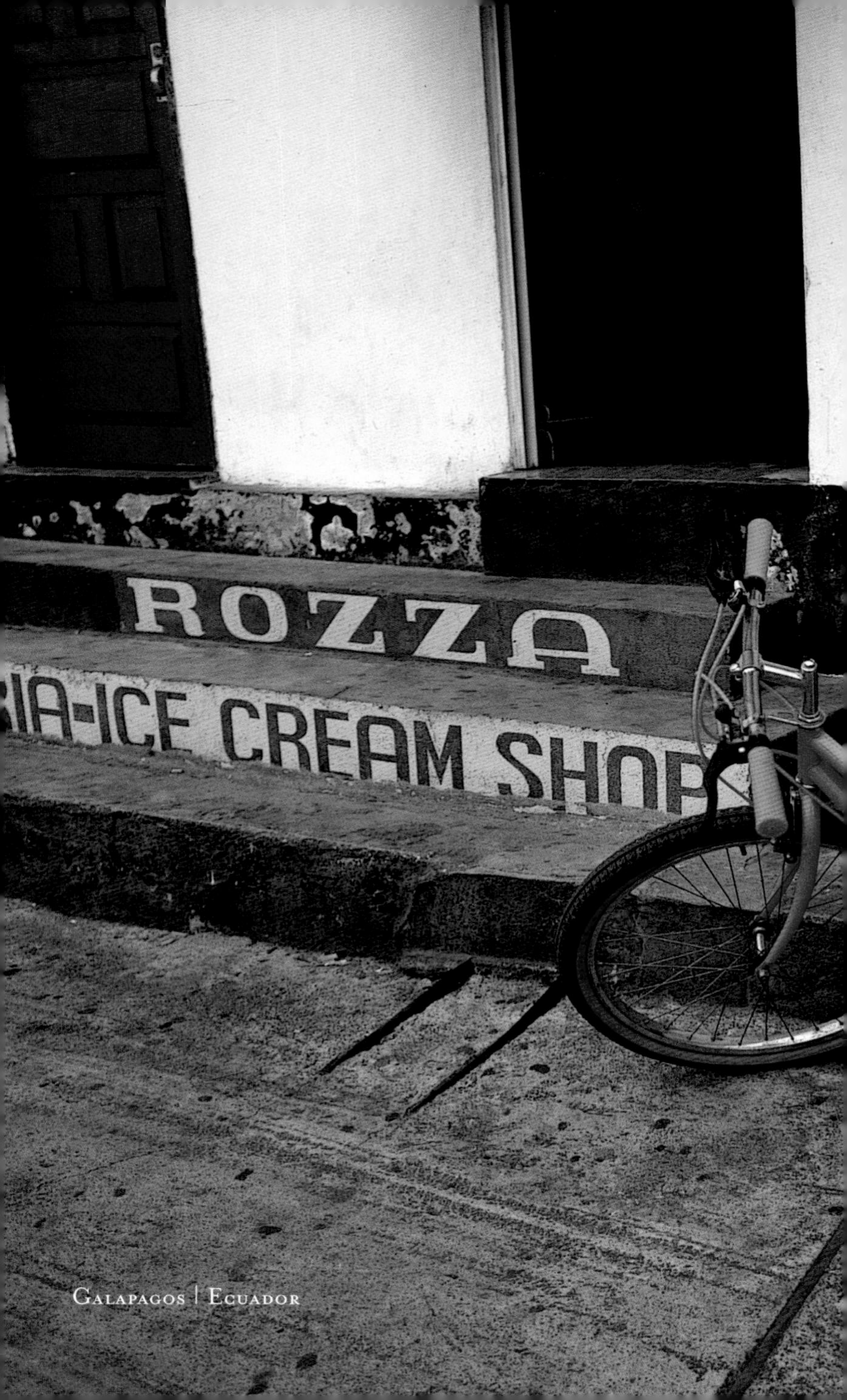
ROZZA
IA-ICE CREAM SHOP
GALAPAGOS | ECUADOR

GALAPAGOS | ECUADOR

ROME | ITALY

.

BATH | ENGLAND

RADZIWILL ESTATE | POLAND

Vienna | Austria

Outskirts of Copenhagen | Denmark

Overleaf: Konya | Turkey

BEIJING | CHINA

JAVA | INDONESIA

Fez | Morocco

Chiloé | Chile

Berkeley | California

CAIRNS | AUSTRALIA